ANIMALS IN DANGER!

Sea Otters

Nancy Dickmann

BROWN BEAR BOOKS

Published by Brown Bear Books Ltd
4877 N. Circulo Bujia
Tucson, AZ 85718
USA

and

Unit 1/D, Leroy House
436 Essex Rd
London N1 3QP
UK

ISBN 978-1-78121-445-9 (library bound)
ISBN 978-1-78121-467-1 (paperback)

Library of Congress Cataloging-in-Publication Data available on request

Text: Nancy Dickmann
Designer: Supriya Sahai
Design Manager: Keith Davis
Picture Researcher: Laila Torsun
Editorial Director: Lindsey Lowe
Children's Publisher: Anne O'Daly

Manufactured in the United States of America
CPSIA compliance information: Batch#AG/5623

Picture Credits

The photographs in this book are used by permission and through the courtesy of:

Front Cover: FLPA: Suzi Eszterhas/Minden Pictures
Alamy: Milo Burcham 12–13; Doc White/Nature Picture Library 8–9; iStock: Phil Augustavo 18–19, brunette 14–15, Ken Canning 1, 21, J. Clegg 7, Dougall Photography 18, fdastudillo 8, David Gomez 4, lfness 10, kwiktor 20, laughingmango 16–17; NaturePL: Doc White 12; Shutterstock: EQRoy 16, Christian Musta 14, Menno Schaefer 4–5; SPL: Thomas and Pat Leeson 10–11.

All other artwork and photography © Brown Bear Books.

t-top, r-right, l-left, c-center, b-bottom

Brown Bear Books has made every attempt to contact the copyright holder. If you have any information please contact: licensing@brownbearbooks.co.uk

Websites

The website addresses in this book were valid at the time of going to press. However, it is possible that contents or addresses may change following publication of this book. No responsibility for any such changes can be accepted by the author or the publisher. Readers should be supervised when they access the Internet.

Words in **bold** appear in the Useful Words on page 23.

Contents

What Are Sea Otters?

Sea otters are furry animals. They are related to weasels and river otters. But sea otters live in the oceans. They are expert swimmers.

Sea otters live in waters near the **coast**.

IN DANGER!
Sea otters are in danger of dying out. People need to protect them.

Sea otters are **mammals**. Their bodies are covered in fur. An adult is as big as a medium-sized dog. Sea otters breathe air. They come to the water's surface to breathe.

Sea Otter Habitats

A **habitat** is the place where an animal lives. Sea otters' habitats are in the northern Pacific Ocean. The water is cold. Sea otters spend most of their time in the water.

Sea otters live near North America and Asia. They do not go far from the **coasts.**

A sea otter's body is built for swimming.
Its back feet are **webbed**. This helps it swim.
The **nostrils** close when a sea otter dives.
An otter's fur is very thick. This keeps it warm.

Finding Food

Sea otters feed in **kelp** forests.
These forests are under the water.
A seaweed called kelp grows there.
Prickly sea urchins eat the kelp.
Sea otters eat the sea urchins.

Many different animals live in kelp forests.

Sea otters catch other animals to eat. They eat squid and octopus. They eat also clams and crabs. Otters catch fish to eat. Claws on their front paws grip slippery fish.

Using Tools

Sea otters eat mussels. They eat other shellfish too. They must crack open the hard shells. Then they can eat the meat inside. Sea otters use stones as tools to crack shells.

Mussels are soft, but they have hard shells.

A sea otter floats on its back. It places a rock on its chest. Then it bangs the mussel against the stone. It keeps hitting until the shell breaks.

WOW!

A sea otter carries its stone when it dives. It stores the stone in a pouch under its arm.

Baby Sea Otters

Baby sea otters are called pups. They are born in the water. They cannot swim at first. The mother wraps the pup in seaweed while she hunts. This keeps the pup from floating away.

The mother floats on her back.
Her baby lies on her chest.
It drinks milk from its mother's body.

Sea Otters in Danger

Some animals are **endangered**.

Long ago, people hunted sea otters.

They used their fur for clothes.

Sea otters were nearly wiped out.

Orcas hunt and eat sea otters.

Sea otters are still in danger. Some get tangled in fishing nets. Many are killed by **oil** spilled in the ocean.

Helping Sea Otters

About 100 years ago, there were only 2,000 sea otters left. In 1911, a law was passed. Countries agreed to stop hunting sea otters.

Sea otters need clean water. Cleaning up the ocean helps sea otters.

Scientists count sea otters.
They check if they are healthy.
Some **diseases** affect sea otters.
Scientists look for cures.

What's Next?

After the 1911 law, sea otters started to recover. Now there are more than 100,000 sea otters. But their numbers are falling again.

In a few places, sea otters are doing well.

WOW!

Some businesses farm shellfish. They do not want sea otters nearby.

People use the oceans for fishing. They drill for **oil**. They take part of the sea otters' **habitat**. If the habitat gets too small, sea otters might die out. People need to protect sea otters.

Sea Otter Helpers

These groups help sea otters:

The International Union for Conservation of Nature (IUCN) is a group of scientists. The scientists count animals. They keep track of their numbers. They decide whether an animal is **endangered**. They say when it has gone **extinct**.

Friends of the Sea Otter is a charity. It makes sure that laws protect sea otters.

Monterey Bay Aquarium rescues sea otters. Scientists give them radio collars. This helps them track the otters.

Fact File

Average life span: up to 23 years

Length: 4 feet (1.22 m)

Weight: 65 pounds (29 kg)

Diet: mainly fish and shellfish

Dives: up to 270 feet (82 m) deep

WOW!

Sea otters often sleep holding paws with another otter. This keeps them from drifting away.

Try It!

Imagine that you are a scientist. You are counting sea otters in a local bay. You want to see if they are in danger. You can make a graph.

You will need:

- graph paper
- pencil
- ruler

Year	Sea Otters
2000	25
2005	24
2010	19
2015	21

1 Write "Date" at the bottom of the graph. Write the years on the line. They should be evenly spaced.

2 Along the side, write "Sea otter numbers." Write in numbers from 15 to 25.

3 Use the data in the table to plot the numbers on the graph.

4 Use the ruler to connect the dots. Are sea otter numbers going up or down?

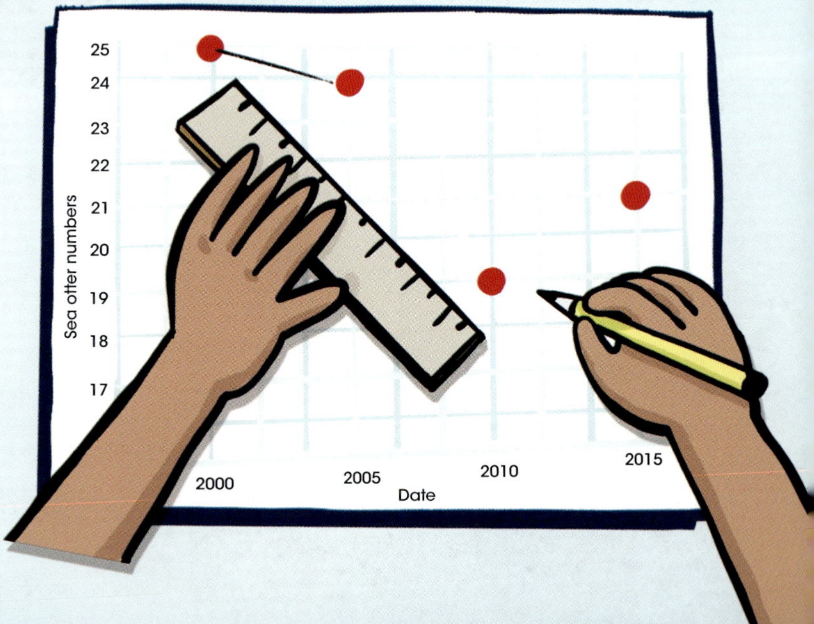

Useful Words

coast The place where the land meets the sea.

disease A serious illness.

endangered In danger of dying out completely so that no more are left.

extinct Having died out completely so that no more are left.

habitat The place where a plant or animal lives.

kelp A type of seaweed. It is attached to the ocean floor. Kelp can form underwater "forests."

mammal Member of a group of animals that have fur and make milk for their young.

nostrils The openings in the nose where air goes in or out.

oil A thick, black, sticky liquid found underground. It can be made into fuel.

orca Another name for a killer whale, a large black-and-white dolphin.

webbed Having skin connecting the fingers or toes. Webbed feet are good for swimming.

Find Out More

Websites

kids.nceas.ucsb.edu/mmp/seaotter.html

www.monterey-bayaquarium.org/animals-and-experiences/live-web-cams/sea-otter-cam

www.national-geographic.com/animals/mammals/s/sea-otter/

Books

Sea Otters Laura Marsh, National Geographic Kids, 2014

Sea Otters Nathan Sommer, Bellwether Media, 2018

Sea Otters Louise Spilsbury, Heinemann, 2013

Index